OBJECT LESSONS
FROM NATURE

by

SYLVIA M. MATTSON

MOODY PRESS
CHICAGO

OBJECT LESSONS
FROM NATURE

PREFACE

OBJECT LESSONS FROM NATURE not only reveal some of the wonders of God's creation, but also afford instructors an excellent opportunity to teach the way of salvation in an eye- and heart-catching manner. In addition to using the lessons for Sunday school classes, teachers for summer camps and vacation Bible schools will also find the material in this book helpful. Women, seeking Nature devotional programs, will find that sections in these lessons can be used with only slight adjustment.

Many of the lessons can be used to teach special subjects in Sunday school. For instance, Lesson 3 illustrates Christian growth; Lesson 5, God's protection; Lesson 11, temperance; Lesson 21, forgiveness. Although all of the lessons teach the folly of sin, Lesson 11 is wholly adapted to that subject. Lesson 28 is the Christmas lesson.

The spiritual truths follow each thought of Nature, so as to make it easy to "lift" out parts in each lesson. This feature makes it possible to adjust the lesson length to the time allowed for the

class period. The teacher would need to prepare
a summary to fit the material "lifted" from the lessons. There is a slight overlapping of lesson
thoughts and Bible references, this being done to
help those who teach the lessons out of sequence.

An index to the scriptures is given for the convenience of teachers using the *International Sunday
School Lessons.* Object lesson material can easily
be located through the Bible references shown in
the quarterly.

It is suggested that the lessons be read once or
twice, and then the material be given in the teacher's own words, adding personal experience stories.
A short outline can be made to show the points that
are to be used.

CONTENTS

7

Lesson 1

THE SMALLER PLANTS

OBJECT NEEDED: A plant.

Plants are everywhere, from the North Pole to the South Pole. Some plants like to live in the cold arctic while others prefer the scorching and humid equator. There are plants for the deserts, plants for the swamps, plants for the oceans, and plants for the land. Some of them are so small that one needs a microscope to see them, while others, like the redwood trees, are huge and very tall. In a later lesson we'll talk about the larger plants, such as trees. Most plants manufacture their own food, however, there are a few, called parasites, that actually rob their neighbors. Also, there are plants that eat insects, the Venus's-flytrap being one of them.

Plants have two names, just as do all people. Your last name may be Jones and your first name John. (Teacher may use names from the class.) At home you are known as John, but in school you are registered by both of your names—John Jones. Now, let's see how the two-name system fits the plant. All oak trees are named *Quercus,* but only the white oak is *Quercus alba.* The swamp white oak is a brother to the white oak, and it must have a "given" name to go with the family of oaks. Thus, its full name is *Quercus bicolor.* You will notice that the individual name (species) comes last, with the oak family name being first. This method is reverse of the way humans write their name. Sometimes people have nicknames. In the plant kingdom we have what is called a "common name." The common name for *Quercus alba* is White Oak. (If there is a blackboard in the room, write the names on the board.)

Let's take a look at this plant that we have before us. As you know, this plant needs a number of "essentials" in order to live. One of the very important things that it needs is light. If there was no light on this earth, plants could not exist. We could not exist either. The sun provides light and the leaves of the plant transfer the sunlight into energy. It is through this energy that the plant grows instead of dying. Christ is the Light of the World, and it's through Him that we receive Eternal Life. Jesus said, "I am the light of the world: he that followeth me shall not walk in darkness, but shall have the light of life" (John 8:12). When we accept Jesus as our Saviour, the Light causes us to grow spiritually.

A plant also needs water. This small plant would not live very long if I did not water it. When we fail to water our lawn, the grass dries up and dies. Spiritually speaking, Christ is the Water of Life, and it's through Him "we live and have our being." The Bible says: "Whosoever drinketh of the water that I shall give him shall never thirst; but the water that I shall give him shall be in him a well of water springing up into everlasting life" (John 4: 14).

Plants also need food. We sometimes "feed" our lawns to get them to grow fast. Some plants, like the banana, grow very fast. The banana can be cut down, and in a matter of a few hours it has again grown into a small "tree." There are some people who grow more rapidly spiritually than others. God not only gives us the Light, and the Water of Life; but He also gives us food to make us grow fast spiritually. The Christian receives "food" through Bible study and prayer. When these two "essentials" are omitted, the Christian becomes "dried up."

Temperature has much to do with the growth of a plant. You may have heard the farmer say that he can "hear" the corn grow on warm nights. There are many plants that cannot stand cold weather. The first night of frost kills them. There is also a temperature to Christian living. The cold church member is of no help to Christ. Neither does Christ want members who are only lukewarm. In the Book of Revelation we find this verse: "I know thy works, that thou art neither cold nor hot: I would thou wert cold or hot. So then because thou art lukewarm, and neither cold nor hot, I will spue thee out of my mouth" (Rev. 3:15, 16). The people who were "hot" were the ones who lived out-and-out for Christ. The ones who were "cold" were not interested in working for the Lord. There is a definite division between those that are "hot" and those that are "cold." Those that are "lukewarm" are on the fence, as we might say. The church member who has a "hot" Christian experience is the one God can use.

Plants are very useful to mankind. Many of them provide food and medicine. They provide many chemicals; and of course such drinks as tea, coffee, cola, and chocolate also come from plants. Cotton and linen material is made possible by plant life. God made plants to be useful to man. Men were created to be useful to God. Many men are never of any use to God, because they continue to live in sin. There are many, however, who become Christians, and these shoulder the duties that God gives them. They spread the Gospel by preaching (II Tim. 4:2), by teaching (Matt. 28:19), and by witnessing (Isa. 43:10). These Christians are helpful to humanity by the kind and useful deeds that they do (I Peter 3:8; Rom. 12:10).

Plants need a proper location in which to grow. Sandy soil suits some of them, while others like a loamy ground. Plants that grow in the ocean cannot grow on land, and those that grow on the land would not live very long if placed in the ocean. Can you imagine a farmer planting corn in the ocean! Each Christian has his "proper place" to serve God. God may place one of you in Africa, while he might ask another to live in China. Some of you will work for the Lord in this country. There is a "location" for each Christian.

Sometimes good plants have a difficult time to live because there are so many weeds to crowd them out. There are also insects that like to eat the leaves. The Devil would like to have bad habits crowd out the good ones. He also wants the Christian to omit Bible reading, so that God's word cannot take root. Sin acts like a weed or a bad insect when it is allowed to exist.

Plants have other enemies—such as heavy winds, floods, hail, freezing weather and heat. Man is also an enemy to the plant because he uses it for food. Thus, we see that plants have a constant struggle in order to live. The Christian also has a constant struggle against the Devil and un-Christian associates. The Bible says: "Put on the whole armour of God, that ye may be able to stand against the wiles of the devil. . . Submit yourselves therefore to God. Resist the devil, and he will flee from you" (Eph. 6:11; James 4:7).

I'm wondering if you have ever heard of "plant communities." Should we say that certain plants like each other's company so well that they grow together? A small pond or marsh may hold cattails, horsetails, and lilies. Ferns, mosses, lichens, and mushrooms like to live together in a heavy wooded area. Plants grow together, not because they like each other, but because they want the same growing conditions. Christians, because they have the same interests in life, enjoy each other's company. If we're real Christians, we will want to associate with other Christians rather than with unbelievers. The members of the early Church, as pictured in the New Testament, liked each other's company so well that they actually lived together. Being together was good for them, because they grew spiritually, and added daily to their group (Acts 2:47).

There are many scientific improvements that help plants to be healthy and to grow more abundantly. God has "improvements" that help us to be better

Christians. A "closer walk with Jesus" is one of these improvements. Others are: Bible reading, prayer, Christian associates, and clean habits.

Most plants do the will of the person who planted them. Occasionally we find one that goes "astray." Christians should always do the will of their Heavenly Father. There are some Christians who have a mind of their own and do not want to follow the leading of the Heavenly Father. The Bible says: "This is the way, walk ye in it" (Isa. 30:21). Can you say by your deeds and words that you are walking in the will of your Heavenly Father?

Lesson 2

TREES

OBJECTS NEEDED: A branch from a deciduous tree and one from a conifer.

In today's lesson we're going to talk about trees in general. Later we will have a lesson on the various parts of the tree. The Bible mentions many kinds of trees that we have in our land today. It also mentions the tree of life (Gen. 2:9) and the tree of knowledge (Gen. 2:17). There is also the tree that was made into a cross for Christ to bear our sins (I Peter 2:24).

A tree has a trunk, from which extend branches like the ones we have here. A tree also has leaves which manufacture its food. A tree could not live if it did not have any leaves. It also has roots, blossoms and fruit. How long do you think a tree could exist if it refused to have leaves, refused to have flowers, refused to have fruit? Trees don't act that way! People are the ones in God's creation that have such behavior. Many Christians refuse to bear fruit for the Lord Jesus Christ. By bearing fruit we mean that they do not work for their Lord. They keep their time and money to themselves, and they do not give God His share of either of them.

Although all trees have trunks, roots, leaves, blossoms, and fruit, yet we cannot say that they are alike. We have two types of trees illustrated here this morning. One of these contains broad leaves, which drop in the fall. The other tree contains needles which stay green all winter. The tree that drops its leaves is called deciduous and the one with the needles is called conifer, or evergreen. When the deciduous tree drops its leaves, it takes a rest. Since the leaves manufacture the food for the tree, the tree becomes dormant. The conifer is green the whole year through. Sometimes Christians take a rest—they allow others to do the church work. They do not manufacture any energy for the Lord's work. There are other Christians who keep working for the Lord the year around. They are alive all the time, and do not take a rest. These working Christians are like the evergreen tree which keeps green the year around.

Trees are identified by their leaves, flowers, fruits, bark, and the shape of the tree. Later, when we have a lesson on leaves, we'll find out there are many kinds of them to help identify the trees. There are other ways of knowing a tree. The birch is identified by its white bark; the pine is known for its needles and its cones; the hazelnut or the alder is identified by its catkins. Fruits are an excellent identification. We know that apples do not grow on a peach tree.

Thus, we see that trees are individuals, each with a specific kind of leaf, bark, flower, and fruit. You boys and girls are also individuals in God's sight. He knows each one of you by name, and He knows what you are capable of doing for Him if you will give Him your heart.

Trees have various shapes. The white bark pine found on Timberline at Mt. Hood is so wind torn that it hugs the ground and does not grow upright, making it the most photographed object of nature at Timberline. The tree is so ugly that it actually is beautiful. How many Christians are ugly in appearance; but, because of their sweet and loving disposition, they become beautiful to others. The scars on their faces are not noticed, nor are their deformities a handicap.

The tree is anchored by its roots. When the wind blows, the tree sways but does not fall because its roots hold it in place. If its roots are not deep, the tree may blow over. The Devil would like to sway you off your feet by winds of unbelief; but if you're anchored in the Word of God, you will have good roots to withstand the temptations of the Devil.

Trees are the largest of all God's creations. Some trees are three hundred feet high, and a few are even more! Imagine being that tall! They are also the oldest of living things. They are the only living things that continue to have birthdays after birthdays, until they have had a thousand or more of them. The age of the General Sherman tree is estimated at 3,500 years. When we have a birthday, we generally make a fuss about it and then someone gives us a present. Of course, some people omit a few birthdays, if they don't want their friends to know how old they are. The tree makes no fuss over its birthdays—it just quietly stands, offering shade and beauty to all. It is seen but seldom heard, unless we have a storm. There are many Christians who work quietly for the Lord. They don't go around "blowing" about their accomplishments—they let someone else do the talking about them (Prov. 27:2).

Trees are useful—they provide fruits for us to eat. We enjoy apples, peaches, pears, and other fruits. We also like to eat walnuts, almonds, filberts, and other nuts. The tree is also useful in the building of homes and furniture. Sometimes the tall poplars are used as wind breakers around farm houses. The sap from such trees as the maple is used as food. There is one usefulness that all trees have in common—they provide shade on hot days.

The Lord would want each of you boys and girls to be useful to Him. He would want you to spread the Gospel by inviting your friends to Sunday school and by speaking to them about Jesus.

Trees are beautiful. In the spring the trees have large green leaves that offer cool shade. In the fall we admire the yellow and red coloring that has so suddenly appeared. The lofty and stately beauty of the trees have inspired man in various ways. Sometimes summer camps make "outdoor cathedrals" under the trees. Their massive forms help to draw worshipers close to God. Christians, by their actions and words, can excite others to reverence. Do you know of men and women who, because of their Christian influence, will cause rough and profane people to cease their swearing and vile talking when they are around? Your life can be like a tall tree, standing as a Christian symbol to those who do not know the Lord Jesus Christ.

The Bible mentions trees talking to each other (Judges 9:8-15). We have heard them singing when the wind blows through them (I Chron. 16:33). Because of the shapes of the leaves, the broad-leaf tree has a different song from that of the conifer. The tree is able to give a message to man without saying a word. When the leaves appear in the spring, we can almost hear the tree say, "Spring is here—get busy and do your planting." Later, when the air becomes hot, we can imagine it would say, "Summer is here—relax in my shade." When the leaves start to drop in the autumn, the tree seems to say, "Fall is here—get ready for winter." Thus, we see the tree has a message for each season, and the Bible says: "To every thing there is a season, and a time to every purpose under the heaven: a time to be born, and a time to die; a time to plant, and a time to pluck up that which is planted" (Eccles. 3: 1, 2). There is only one season for giving out the Gospel—and that is the whole year through. Christians plant the seed of Jesus in the hearts of the sinner. God "waters" the seed, and then there is a harvest when the unbeliever gives his heart to the Lord Jesus Christ.

A tree grows each year. If we were to place a nail into a young tree just three feet up on the trunk, we'd find that in ten years that the nail was still three feet up on the trunk. Then how does the tree grow? It adds to its height by its yearly twigs. After their first year of growth these twigs are fixed in length and grow only in thickness. Then the next year another twig appears on the end of the branch and it starts to grow. Year by year the tree adds to its size in this manner. God expects His children to grow spiritually each year. The Bible says: "Grow in grace, and in the knowledge of our Lord and Saviour Jesus Christ"

(II Peter 3:18). "The righteous shall flourish like the palm tree: he shall grow like a cedar in Lebanon" (Ps. 92:12).

Have you added to your life by reading your Bible and by praying? Have you grown through attendance at Sunday school and church services? God would like to have you grow spiritually, just as the tree grows from day to day.

Lesson 3

LEAVES

OBJECTS NEEDED: An assortment of deciduous leaves of various sizes and shapes.

A tree could not live if it were not for its leaves. They are sometimes called the chemical lab of the tree. The trees and smaller plants are the only living things in God's creation that are capable of making their own food. That is the reason for calling the leaves the chemical lab of the tree. Man must have plant or animal life in order to survive. He cannot manufacture his food like plants can. The animals must also have plants, and in some cases they require the lives of smaller animals than themselves.

When the sun shines upon a leaf, the green coloring matter (called chlorophyll) causes a chemical change to take place. The leaf takes in carbon dioxide and sunshine, and unites them with water that it receives from the roots; and then it manufactures food, which we call sugar. We have an unlimited supply of carbon dioxide in the air and

23

we have plenty of water, and the world is full of sunshine; but we do not have an over abundance of sugar. Scientists cannot understand how the plant can manufacture sugar. This chemical lab that is located in the leaf is very baffling.

God has many mysteries in His creation. We do not understand how a sinful person can suddenly become a respectable man. In fact there are times in which we cannot understand why God would want any of us around because of our wayward-ness. God says: "Thou hast wearied me with thine iniquities" (Isa. 43:24). He, nevertheless, does not forsake us.

We have spoken of the leaf as a chemical lab. In order for a leaf to manufacture food it has to be attached to the plant. This leaf that I hold in my hand is no longer a chemical lab, because it is de-tached from the stem. In a few hours it will wither and die. When you became a Christian, you at-tached yourself to Jesus Christ. It's through Him that you receive the nourishment necessary for your spiritual life. Those who have not attached them-selves to Jesus are spiritually dead. But God can remove the sin so that each of them can become His follower. The Bible says: "And you hath he quickened, who were dead in trespasses and sins" (Eph. 2:1).

The leaf is attached to the stem for one purpose—

that of supplying food to the plant. The Christian boy or girl has one reason for existing—to win other boys and girls for Christ.

Leaves perspire when the day is hot. A large oak tree may throw off as much as fifty barrels of water in a day. The Christian throws off kindness, meekness, gentleness, etc. (See Gal. 5:22, 23.)

Leaves, as we have already mentioned, must have sunshine. The leaves are arranged on the tree so that the sun will reach each of them. If the sun does not reach a leaf, it will adjust itself so as to reach the light. We should not allow anything to get in the way of receiving the Gospel Light. God has enough Light for all of us, if we will "adjust" our lives so as to receive it.

Today we're going to study the detail of these leaves we have before us. You can see that not all these leaves are of the same size, or of the same shape. Leaves may be very, very small, probably a fraction of an inch; or they may be very large— palm leaves are 50 to 60 feet long. There may be only a few leaves on a tree as the palm, while the poplar may have 70,000 and an oak 700, 000. Leaves may be long and narrow, as the willow; or they may be long and wider as the elm and the alder. They may be heart-shaped as the cottonwood, or triangular as the aspen. Some leaves, such as the oak and maple, may have lobes. The leaves can also be compound, such as the ash. Thus, we see that leaves are individuals. (If possible, have samples to show the different forms of leaves.)

All people are individuals. Some are white, while others are yellow or black. They may be short, tall, fat, or skinny. You are an individual in God's sight. God knows what you are able to do for Him, and how much He can depend upon you.

Some leaves are attached close to the stem, while others have a stalk. Some Christians live close to Christ and try to do His will; while others do not want to live close because they want their own way.

In the fall, the trees scatter their leaves around their base, and then they go to sleep for the winter. Thus, we see that leaves are here for only a season. Christians do not live on this earth very long before God calls them home. We say we're here for "a season."

As we think of the function of the leaf, we have to admit that this part of the tree is a real worker. The leaf doesn't shout about the work that it is doing. It just works and works. When the leaves on a tree become poisoned or infested with harmful insects, they may die. If all of the leaves die, the tree will also die. You are God's worker. He is depending upon you to keep the Gospel from dying in your neighborhood. Can God depend upon you just as the tree depends upon the leaf?

Lesson 4

LOOKING AT THE INSIDE
OF A TREE

OBJECTS NEEDED: Cut a cross section of a tree to show its annual rings. Also, cut a longitudinal section to show how the lines run up and down inside of the tree.

Some of you may have cut wood for a bonfire. Have you ever examined these pieces of wood to see what the inside of a tree looked like? I have here a cross section of a tree. Notice the rings that are in it. If I counted these rings I could find out the age of this tree. This other piece shows lines running up and down in the tree. It shows the veins that carry the food and water from the roots to the leaves.

The tree grows wider each year as shown by the annual rings. There is one of these rings added each year. The growth of a tree, as indicated by the annual rings, is only visible on the inside. We are unable to know the age of this tree without cutting it down and looking inside. God cannot tell how much we have grown spiritually in the past year without looking inside of us. He checks our hearts in order to determine our spiritual growth. Our growth is measured by prayer (Luke 18:1; Rom. 12:12), Bible reading (Ps. 119:12, 18, 33; II Tim. 2:15), Christian fellowship (Heb. 10:25; Col. 3:16), praise (Ps. 34:1), stewardship (Mal. 3:10), and faith (Luke 17:5). Our spiritual growth is likened unto a tree: "The righteous shall flourish like the palm tree: he shall grow like a cedar in Lebanon . . . I am like a green olive tree in the house of God . . . for he shall be as a tree planted by the waters, and that spreadeth out her roots by the river, and shall not see when heat cometh, but her leaf shall be green; and shall not be careful in the year of drought, neither shall cease from yielding fruit" (Ps. 92:12; Ps. 52:8; Jer. 17:8).

The tree accurately tells its age by the annual rings. It's not like people who fib about their age for a special purpose. We cannot fool God on our spiritual growth. He is able to tell accurately what our growth has been each year.

The tree not only tells its age, but it also has embodied in its trunk a vast amount of history. It tells of the dry years by its narrow rings, and it indicates the moist years by the broad rings. The trees gave the answer as to why the Indian cliff dwellers left the Southwest. The historians found, by checking the rings in the trees, that there was a severe drought in the last part of the 13th century. The giant trees of the West show history in the making in the years in which Christ appeared upon the earth. Many of the Sequoia trees are from 4,000 to 5,000 years old. There are hardships, other than drought, that are registered in the tree trunks. The tree may tell us by a nail embedded in the wood, that its owner had a fence hooked to it but later ripped it off, overlooking to remove the nail. There have been times in which court cases relating to boundaries have been settled because of the story told by a tree.

Our life also shows our Christian hardships. It will reveal the persecution that caused us to lose faith in God. It will show the bad habit that entered and held us bound like a slave. Our life will also show the love we have for God—the way we have worshiped, prayed, and worked. Some of our Christian history is visible to our friends. What is visible to God is the most important.

As you look inside of your life this morning, can you see a good Christian growth—a growth that is pleasing to God? The Bible says: "Grow in grace, and in the knowledge of our Lord and Saviour Jesus Christ" (II Peter 3:18).

If you are not growing, take a look at your life.

Do you have bad habits that hinder the growth? Do you have evil thoughts, followed by un-Christian action? God can remove all of these hindrances from your life. The Bible says: "He that covereth his sins shall not prosper: but whoso confesseth and forsaketh them shall have mercy . . . if we confess our sins, he is faithful and just to forgive us our sins, and to cleanse us from all unrighteousness" (Prov. 28:13; I John 1:9).

Lesson 5

BARK

OBJECTS NEEDED: Use same cross section of a tree that was required in Lesson No. 4. This piece of wood should show the outer protection of bark. Also, have a piece of thick rough bark.

The bark on a young tree is generally green and smooth, and contains sap. When the tree becomes older, the bark is broken into irregular ridges, forming deep furrows, and contains no sap. The furrows could remind us of the wrinkles on one's face as age creeps up. As we examine this piece of bark, we notice its coarse ridges which cross and form a net-mesh design. The cross section of wood that we have before us shows the position of the bark in relation to the other sections. The bark is on the outside and protects the tree.

We can drive a nail into the bark of a full grown tree without injury to the tree. Since there is no sap flowing through the bark, the nail does not damage the tree. This outer coating protects the

tree in other ways. For instance, the bark shields
the tree from extreme changes in temperature. Before a tree can "freeze" the cold air must first get
through the bark. The bark also assists in reducing
evaporation of water from the tissues inside of the
tree.

Jesus is the bark around our lives. He is our
protector. "O Lord, thou art my God; I will exalt
thee, I will praise thy name; for thou hast done
wonderful things . . . for thou has been a strength
to the poor, a strength to the needy in his distress,
a refuge from the storm, a shadow from the heat,
when the blast of the terrible ones is as a storm
against the wall" (Isa. 25:1, 4). The Lord says:
"I the Lord have called thee in righteousness, and
will hold thine hand, and will keep thee" (Isa.
42:6).

Sometimes people carve their initials in the bark.
The outer coating of the hackberry has proved a
temptation to many boys. These carvings do not
kill the tree, because the bark serves as a protector.
But the carvings deface the tree, giving it a hor-
rible appearance. There are people who "deface"
the name of Jesus. They "carve" unsightly remarks
into His name. Let's look at a few that are mentioned in the Bible. Swearing by God's name is a
favorite "carving." The Bible says: "Thou shalt
not take the name of the Lord thy God in vain;

for the Lord will not hold him guiltless that taketh his name in vain" (Exod. 20:7). "My name continually every day is blasphemed" (Isa. 52:5). Also, there will be teachers and others who will "poke fun" at God's Word in your presence, especially if you are a Christian. The Bible says: "There shall come in the last days scoffers, walking after their own lusts, and saying, Where is the promise of his coming?" (II Peter 3:3, 4). Have you heard people make remarks like these: "So you believe in the Bible, eh? And you think Jesus will come again to this earth? Why don't you get on a satellite and start looking for Him?" Remarks like these are constantly being thrown at you boys and girls in school. Let's remember it is not possible to kill a tree by carving into the bark, nor can immoral and profane people kill your belief in God so long as you allow Jesus to stand guard around you. The Psalmist said, "It is God that girdeth me with strength, and maketh my way perfect" (Ps. 18:32).

The bark on a tree is useful as medicine. Cascara bark is used much in the preparation of tonics. Jesus, the "Bark" around our lives, contains the medicine that can heal a sin-sick soul (Luke 5:20). Christ's medicine also heals sorrow and grief (Rev. 21:4).

Just as the bark is useful for many things, Christ is also useful to us in many ways. First of all, He is our guide. "The Lord shall guide thee continually" (Isa. 58:11). We need to say: "For thou art my rock and my fortress; therefore for thy name's sake lead me, and guide me" (Ps. 31:3). The Lord also provides for our physical needs. "Wherefore, if God so clothe the grass of the field, which today is, and tomorrow is cast into the oven, shall he not much more clothe you, O ye of little faith?" (Matt. 6:30). Bark has been used much in the preparation of dye. Christ is also useful to us in dying. We spell the word differently, however, and with a change of meaning. We shall have everlasting life after our physical death (John 3:16).

In some instances the bark on a tree is a means of identification. We recognize the birch by its white bark. We also identify the cedar by its bark which flakes off in long narrow strips. When you accepted Jesus as your Saviour, He placed an identification tag upon you. You took His name, forming your new name of *Christ*ian. Christ's standard of purity has been transferred to your life. Have you this identification tag upon your life? Has the Lord said: "I have called thee by thy name: thou art mine" (Isa. 43:1)? You can have Him if you are willing to confess your sins and ask Him to be your Saviour. The Bible says: "He that covereth his sins shall not prosper: but whoso confesseth

and forsaketh them shall have mercy" (Prov. 28:
13). Are you willing to say: "I acknowledged my
sin unto thee, and mine iniquity have I not hid.
I will confess my transgressions unto the Lord; and
thou forgavest the iniquity of my sin" (Ps. 32:5)?

Why don't you take Christ this morning as *your*
Saviour?

Lesson 6

ROOTS

OBJECTS NEEDED: Dig up a variety of weeds, washing the roots thoroughly. If a rye plant is available, bring its main roots to class. A carrot or a beet should also be used.

Today we're going to talk about roots. Can you tell me what are roots? Why do plants have them? (Allow the class an opportunity to give their answers.)

I have brought two common types of root systems to class. The one is called diffuse (fibrous) root system. This type of system contains numerous main roots, usually slender, with many smaller root branches. Wheat, corn, rye, and other grasses have this kind of root. The other type of root system is known as tap-root. The main primary root is larger and longer. Carrots, beets, and dandelions have tap-root systems.

When a plant is pulled up, part of its roots stay in the ground. The root hairs are so fine that they remain in the soil when the plant is removed. It has been estimated that one rye plant will have 6,500 miles of root hairs. That's more than twice the distance from New York City to Portland, Oregon. The main roots of a full-grown rye plant will total nearly 400 miles, and these roots will live in a surface area of 2,500 square feet! It is not possible for all of the roots to be visible when we dig up a plant.

We could say that the members of this church (name your own church) are its root system. Some of the roots, like the minister and the teachers are visible; but there are many behind-the-scene workers. There are the prayer-warriors, those that arrange the flowers, those that clean the church, and many others. These people are not always visible. Nevertheless, these behind-the-scene members are very important to a church's root system. We cannot estimate the "surface" covered by the root system of our church. We're God's root system, whereby the world will be evangelized.

If we were to inspect the tip of a root under a microscope, we'd see that each tiny root has a tough little cap at the end. This cap has a slippery coating on it, so that it can push through the soil. The cap also serves as a protective armor. Each Christian is given a protective armor by God. So long as we're under God's protection, we can go anywhere He sends us. The Devil is limited to what he can do against us. God has said: "I the Lord have called thee in righteousness, and will hold thine hand, and will keep thee" (Isa. 42:6).

In a previous lesson we learned that the color green was important to the leaf, because it is the sign of life. When we look at these roots, we notice that they are mainly colorless. The tap-roots, like the carrot and the beet, have color in them. When we look at a plant, we do not see the roots. We may notice its gay blossom or its oddly shaped green leaf, but we do not see its colorless roots. When we attend a service at our church, we see the minister, the members of the choir, and the ushers. These workers are the flowers of our church plant. They are the ones who are visible. The roots go deeper. These "roots" may be the bed-fast members who pray, and are not visible.

Now let's look for a few moments at the purpose of roots. The roots absorb water and dissolve minerals from the soil. The water and minerals are important for plant growth. The Christian also needs food for spiritual growth. He receives this food through prayer, Bible study, good books, sermons, radio programs, and association with other Christians.

The tap-roots (like the carrot and beet) are a storage plant. The carrot and the beet stores much food to be used by the plant later. Let's cut open this carrot and take a look at it. Notice, that the center part is different from the outer part. The inside core is the tube through which water and food passes to the plant. The food is stored mainly in the outer layer, which is darker in color. The Christian stores up scripture to keep from sinning: "Thy word have I hid in mine heart, that I might not sin against thee" (Ps. 119:11). We also store up scripture for use in witnessing: "I will speak of thy testimonies also before kings, and will not be ashamed" (Ps. 119:46). Christ found the Scripture to be useful when He wanted to fight the Devil (Matt. 4:4, 7, 10). "So shall I have wherewith to answer him that reproacheth me: for I trust in thy word" (Ps. 119:42). We also have a storehouse that supplies our daily spiritual need. This storehouse is kept full by our Lord.

Our last thought that we want to mention regarding a root is that it anchors the plant to the ground. The wind cannot blow it away from its food and water supply because the roots are hanging on tightly. Its roots penetrate deeply into the earth. The Christian needs to be anchored in the Lord Jesus Christ. The Devil would like to uproot us by the winds of doubt and unbelief, but with a sure Anchor he will not be able to harm us. The Bible says: "Which hope we have as an anchor of

the soul, both sure and stedfast . . . " (Heb. 6:19).
Do you have Christ as your anchor? If you don't,
you can have Him.

Lesson 7

STEMS

OBJECTS NEEDED: Flexible and firm stems, some of which should contain leaves. You should also have grapevine stems and cucumber stems. A knife is necessary also.

We have an assortment of stems before us, from which we're going to receive our lesson. There are many kinds of stems. There are the straight ones that we call the trunk. These thick stems serve as the support for the tree, something similar to the way our backbone holds us up. When we think of the tall and straight stem, we are reminded of a straight, upright Christian. He stands well, and when persecution comes he isn't bounced off his feet. There are many stems that branch off from the trunk of the tree. These stems are not as old as the big stem (trunk) for they have not had time in which to develop. Yet they are part of the "family" of branches. As the trunk grows, it continues to make more stems (branches). All Christians should grow spiritually—they should "branch out," letting their influence show for God.

Another type of stem is produced by the grapevine. (Hold up grapevine stem.) It has climbing stems with tendrils that help it to hang onto a support. A new Christian has to hang onto Jesus and other Christians for support. His life reminds us of the climbing stem.

A third type of stem is produced by the cucumber. (Any stem that sprawls on the ground can be used.) Its long stems sprawl over the ground. It never attempts to elevate itself, but is content to remain in the low level. The people who do not take Jesus into their lives, but instead are content to live in sin, could be called the sprawling type of vine. These people are not capable of supporting themselves, and they need Jesus to pick them up and give them a new life. The Bible says: "If we confess our sins, he is faithful and just to forgive us our sins, and to cleanse us from all unrighteousness" (I John 1:9). If you will confess your sins to Jesus, asking Him to take you as His child, He will lift you up from your life of sin.

The main job assigned stems is that of providing "pipelines" through which water and minerals can come from the soil and pass on their way to the leaves. The stem acts as a pump, always pushing the necessary material up to the leaves. If you were to examine the end of this thick stem, you'd notice different sections in it. (Cut stem with knife.) On the outside there is the bark, which serves as a protection. Then there is the main section, and in the very center there is a spot called the pith. We'll mention the pith later in this lesson. We may wonder how God figured out the structure of a stem, so that the food, water, and minerals would know which channel to use. Apparently, there never is a collision.

Has God a channel in your life through which He can send His Gospel? Does He have a pipeline that sends out kind and helpful words? If you do not have such a channel in your life, you'd better talk to God about it. If your pipeline is full of sin, you'll have to clean it out before your life can be a channel through which God can send His Gospel.

Some stems furnish us with valuable material. The sap of the rubber tree provides rubber, and the pine furnishes turpentine and resin. Sugar syrup comes from the maple tree, and the sap from the chicle tree furnishes chewing gum. If there were no stems, we would not have the sap to furnish us with the products that I have just mentioned. The Christian should also be a producer—he should win others for Christ. Boys and girls have an excellent chance to invite their friends to Sunday school where they will hear the Gospel.

I have a stem here that is very flexible. If I had allowed this stem to remain on the tree, do you think I would be able to bend it in ten years? Stems get thicker as they grow older, and are not flexible. Stiff stems break when they are bent. You boys and girls are like this flexible stem. If you give your heart to the Lord while you are young, God can bend you the way He wants to. When you get older, God may have to break you in order to get His will done.

For a few moments let's return to the thick stem which has been cut so that you can see the inside. You will recall that I mentioned that this center spot was called the pith. Some people call it the heart of the stem. There are naturalists who can identify certain stems by the pith. For instance, the Orgeon Oak has a star-shaped pith. If God looked into your heart, could He identify you as a Christian? God does not look at the outward appearance—He looks into the heart (I Sam. 16:7). Your evil thoughts are visible to God. Your friends may not know your true nature, but God knows it. Let's ask God to cleanse our hearts. "Wash me thoroughly from mine iniquity, and cleanse me from my sin . . . and I shall be whiter than snow" (Ps. 51: 2, 7).

Lesson 8

FLOWERS

OBJECTS NEEDED: Flowers from garden plants, and, if possible, from trees. A pansy is suggested as one of the flowers. Also pick a pansy that has "gone to seed."

We all love flowers. This morning we're going to take a closer look at some of them.

Many of us have the impression that flowers are made solely for beauty and fragrance. But this is not the purpose for which they were created. Flowers are the plant's seed-producing machines. I have here a flower that has already developed its seed. (Open up the pansy ovary to make the seeds visible.)

I have another pansy that has not yet formed seeds. Notice the lines on its petals. Do you know why those lines are there? If you boys had said the lines reminded you of the markings on the airport field, you'd be very close to the correct answer. When the bees visit the flowers to get the honey, they need a place to land. These petals are the

landing field for the bee; and in order for the bee
to know where the honey is, God has made lines
that run to the spot where the honey is located.
Simple, isn't it? Many flowers have a marked landing field for insects. Flowers cannot produce seeds
unless the insects come to get the honey. In the
getting of honey, the bees carry pollen from one
flower to another. The flowers give up honey in
exchange for the pollen that fertilizes the plant.
The bees, of course, are only interested in the
honey. There may be some boy or girl who is looking for a bit of sweetness from your life. A smile
or a kind word may help someone on a rough road.
"Pleasant words are as an honeycomb, sweet to the
soul, and health to the bones" (Prov. 16:24).

Most people plant flowers solely for their beauty.
As we look at these flowers, we can see how beauti-
fully they are colored and shaped. No wonder flowers are taken to the hospitals to cheer those who are
sick. A home is also more cheerful when a bouquet
of flowers is placed on the table. Flowers placed
near the church altar help to produce a worshipful
attitude. As a Christian you can bring cheer to
those sick in sin. They need the help of God to get
rid of their sin; and you, as a Christian, can show
them how to receive this help.

Closely related to the beauty of the flower is its
fragrance. If someone led you into a florist shop

blindfolded, you would know that flowers were near because of the fragrance. There are times in which we can identify the flower by its fragrance. This fact is especially true with the hyacinth. Not all flowers have a pleasing odor. Take, for instance, the skunk cabbage—do people pick it and use it as a bouquet? If they did pick it, they would never repeat their error! The skunk cabbage has an attractive flower and it's too bad that the plant has such an obnoxious odor.

There are people who call themselves Christians, who are offensive to those with whom they work. We could call them the "skunk-cabbage" type of Christian. Their unkind deeds and words embarrass God. They have taken the name Christian, and yet they do not live up to the Christian standard. The real Christian "fragrance" is hard to explain. There are many words that make up the word "fragrance," some of them being kindness, helpfulness, loyalty, co-operation, honesty, friendliness, and many more. As a Christian, are you producing a sweet fragrance for the Lord, or are you offensive because of your actions and speech?

Many plants continue to bloom if the flowers are picked. The pansy will stop blooming if the flowers are allowed to stay on the bush. We then say that the plant has "gone to seed." Have you ever heard someone say, "Oh, that old church member—

he's gone to seed." What do they mean? Could we say he's stopped blooming? That his life no longer radiates with Christian beauty? That he's not interested in working for the Lord? Be sure that you keep the sweet Christian experience God gave you in your youth. Don't allow anyone an opportunity to say that you've "gone to seed."

How long do you think this flower that I'm holding in my hand can live? If it's not placed in water, it will wilt in a few hours. The reason it cannot live is because it's been detached from the plant. The food that the plant sends to its flowers no longer reaches it now that it has been picked. When you became a Christian you attached yourself to Christ. You continue to bloom so long as you stay attached to Christ. Those who run off into sin detach themselves and then their Christian experience becomes wilted.

Flowers are everywhere. Many remote places in the woods contain beautiful flowers. Although no one is there to enjoy the flowers, nevertheless the plant continues to bloom. Let's remember that every thing in Nature lives by expressing itself. When the plant sends forth flowers it is expressing itself. Those who are children of God express themselves in a different manner than those who are living without God. Those who live without God go to sinful places. If you are a Christian you will not want to go to sinful amusement spots. You will express yourself by going to church, by attending Sunday school, and prayer meeting, by doing and saying sweet things, and by fellowshiping with God and other Christians (see Ps. 122:1; Heb. 10:25).

How are you expressing yourself? Do you think God is proud of you as His "flower?" Can you say: "As for me . . . I will serve the Lord" (Josh. 24:15)?

Lesson 9

FRUITS

OBJECTS NEEDED: An assortment of fruit—an apple, orange, nut, a pod of peas or beans.

We have an appetizing object lesson this morning—fruits!

According to the scientist all seed coverings are termed "fruits." The Bible tells us that the seed shall be inside of the fruit: "The fruit tree yielding fruit after his kind, whose seed is in itself" (Gen. 1:11). The scientists are following the Bible statement when they call all seed coverings fruit. Let's cut open this apple, noticing the seed inside. We know that the fruit would look queer if it had its seed on the outside. The birds would come along and take the seed, because there would not be any protection for it. God has placed a fleshy part around the seed, not only to supply us with a delicious fruit, but also to provide a protection for the seed.

Apples, peaches, and pears are pulpy fruits and

are called pomes. Nuts and hard grains of corn, wheat, and oats are dried fruits. Peas and beans are also classed as fruit. The pod with the seeds hanging on one side is called the fruit. With the blackberry or raspberry each tiny compartment is a separate fruit. Likewise, each section of the pineapple is a fruit.

When God created man He gave him the fruits and herbs as food. It wasn't until after the flood that meat was eaten (Gen. 9:3). Although God gave Adam and Eve plenty of fruit from which they could eat, yet they chose to take of the forbidden fruit and thereby sinned (Gen. 2:17). Cain also sinned by offering fruit as a sacrifice to God (Gen. 4:3, 5).

The Bible tells us that, "The fruit tree yielding fruit *after his kind*" (Gen. 1:11). Apples are found on apple trees and peaches grow on peach trees. Of course, we'd know something was wrong if we found apples on the peach trees. The only way they could possibly get on the tree would be for someone to tie them on. God has decreed that trees should bear fruits after their kind, and the decree hasn't changed. The Bible also says: "Ye shall know them by their fruits. Do men gather grapes of thorns, or figs of thistles?" (Matt. 7:16). If you are a Christian you will bear fruits that are becoming a child of God. "The fruit of the Spirit is love, joy, peace, longsuffering, gentleness, goodness, faith, meekness, temperance" (Gal. 5:22, 23) .

Your friends will know if you are a Christian by the fruits which you bear. As a Christian you will not do bad deeds. The Bible says, "A good tree cannot bring forth evil fruit" (Matt. 7:18) . There are people who have corrupt lives, with crime and drunkenness ruling their actions. There are others who pretend they are Christians by trying to do good deeds. But the Bible says: "Neither can a corrupt tree bring forth good fruit" (Matt. 7:18) . "Wherefore by their fruits ye shall know them" (Matt. 7:20) .

In reading our section in Matthew we have skipped a verse. It is not a pleasant verse, but since it is in the Bible we had better read it. "Every tree that bringeth not forth good fruit is hewn down, and cast into the fire" (Matt. 7:19) . If you are not bringing forth good works for the Lord, you should change your way of living. You would not want God to cast you into the fire when you leave this earth. God would like to have you say: "I acknowledged my sin unto thee, and mine iniquity have I not hid. I said, I will confess my transgressions unto the Lord; and thou forgavest the iniquity of my sin" (Ps. 32:5) . If you have not been what God would want you to be, He will forgive you and you can start all over again. "If we confess our sins, he is faithful and just to forgive us our sins, and to cleanse us from all unrighteousness" (I John 1:9).

Lesson 10

SEEDS

OBJECTS NEEDED: An assortment of dry seeds. A few beans should be soaked so that they can be opened for the pupils to see the food stored in them. A bean should be sprouted in moist soil and taken to class and then removed from the soil to show the sprouting. Radish seeds may be sprouted when placed next to a blotter that is between two pieces of glass. A rubber band can hold the glass and blotter together so that it can rest in a dish of water. The sprouted radish seed will be visible through the glass. Odd seeds, like the maple keys, can also be brought to class.

We think of plants and trees as existing for the purpose of supplying us with food; however, if they could talk, they would tell us that they were not made for any such purpose. They have only one purpose—to produce seeds so that more plants can be formed.

Today we have an assortment of seeds before us.

A seed is a tiny package done up in a heavy outside wrapper. This tiny package contains enough food to help the plant get started. When the plant gets its leaves, it is capable of making its own food. I have soaked a few beans so that we can open them and see the food. (Give the beans to the pupils for viewing.) Suppose I were to fill a small jar of beans, pouring water around them, and then place a tight lid on the jar. Do you know what would happen? The jar would break, because the seeds would swell and become powerful enough to break the jar.

Suppose a group of old dried-up Christians decided to cover themselves completely with the Water of Life, Christ Jesus. There would be action! Just as there is life in the seed, so is there life in the dried-up Christian. In each case it takes water to bring action. The seed needs natural water, and the Christian needs a new filling from Christ, the Water of Life.

Inside of this bean is a young plant. So long as the seed remains dry the plant does not grow, but it nevertheless is alive. The plant can remain in the seed for many years. When the seed sprouts it puts forth the tiny leaves stored in the seed. The plant first uses the food that was packed into the seed by the mother plant. Today I have brought a seed that has sprouted in the soil. Let's remove the soil and look at it. You can see how the seed has opened and the plant has started to unfold the leaves that were locked inside the seed. In this glass we have sprouted a few radish seeds between the glass. Notice the roots that have appeared.

By looking at these soaked beans, we have seen the temporary food that God has given the plant. This food lasted only a short time—just long enough for the plant to feed itself. The newly born Christian is like a baby, depending entirely upon God. "As newborn babes, desire the sincere milk of the word, that ye may grow thereby" (I Peter 2:2). God does not want the Christians to continue to live as babies. He wants them to grow. They are expected to start working instead of being pampered and babied by God. "Grow in grace, and in the knowledge of our Lord and Saviour Jesus Christ" (II Peter 3:18).

Plants have many ways in which they spread their seeds. Maple keys have two wings that help the seed to fly. The dandelion has silky parachutes that cause the seed to drift through the air. The jewel weed and touch-me-nots have built-in slingshots that shoot the seed into the air. The squirting cucumbers spread their seeds with their "squirt guns." Some of you may have seen the coconut, which is a very large seed. The coconut is wrapped in a heavy waterproof covering so that it can float on the water. These huge seeds have been known to travel long distances before finding a growing spot. The tumbleweed has one of the most unique and unusual ways of spreading its seeds. When the seeds are ripe, the plant pulls up its roots and starts turning somersaults. As it turns somersaults, it spreads its seeds. Thus, we see there are many ways in which seeds are spread. There are also many ways in which the Gospel is spread. The preacher and Sunday school teachers have their way of giving the Gospel on Sundays. The radio programs have done an unusual amount of spreading the Gospel, reaching many people who do not attend church. Christian books and tracts have also done their part in advancing the kingdom. Personal witnessing was Christ's way of giving the Gospel, and this method is very popular today. God is not particular as to the method we use, so long as we spread the Gospel.

One plant is capable of providing hundreds of seeds. The farmer will tell you that this fact is especially true of weeds! One Christian can help to make many Christians by personal witnessing in word and deed (Ps. 119:46).

Sometimes bad seed gets mixed with the good seed and there is damage done to the harvest. The Bible tells of the mixed seed: "Thou shalt not sow thy field with mingled seed" (Lev. 19:19). If your father is a farmer he may have had some experience with "unclean seed." You boys and girls may have tried to mix bad habits with good ones. You probably learned to your sorrow that the harvest was very poor. If you have mixed badness into your life, you need to say: "Wash me thoroughly from mine iniquity, and cleanse me from my sin . . . Create in me a clean heart, O God; and renew a right spirit within me" (Ps. 51:2, 10).

There are many sizes of seed. The coconut is a very large seed, and the mustard seed is one of the smaller ones. The Bible speaks of the mustard seed: "The kingdom of heaven is like to a grain of mustard seed, which a man took, and sowed in his field: which indeed is the least of all seeds: but when it is grown, it is the greatest among herbs, and becometh a tree, so that the birds of the air come and lodge in the branches thereof" (Matt. 13:31, 32). (It may prove helpful to secure a picture of a grown mustard tree to show the class.) Just a little seed, but think of the size of the tree into which it grows. Small deeds done by boys and girls can do much to help God. These deeds grow through the years and we're surprised at the "big results."

We all know that seeds have to be planted before they can grow into a new plant. They have to be placed into the ground in order for them to have a chance to multiply. God plants His Spirit within us. By our witnessing, the Christians multiply. "Ye are my witnesses, saith the Lord, and my servant whom I have chosen" (Isa. 43:10). It is a wonderful thing to be chosen of God, to help in the spreading of the Gospel. Just as the seed multiplies, will you let your life multiply for God? Let's remember that the harvest is always greater than the seed!

Lesson 11

WEEDS

OBJECTS NEEDED: An assortment of weeds.

We have before us a bunch of weeds. (Name them if you know what they are commonly called.) We don't like weeds because they prevent the growth of the good plants in our garden. Some of you boys and girls may have lived on a farm, and you have had to hoe out the weeds. You can truly say that you don't like them!

What is a weed? (Allow the pupils an opportunity to answer.) You may have heard someone say that a weed is any plant that the farmer doesn't like. Others say weeds are plants with harmful, or objectionable habits. We generally think of weeds as having aggressive tendencies, living where we'd like to see good plants grow. Weeds remind us of sin. There are "harmful and objectionable habits" in the lives of the sinner. Like the weed, sin also has aggressive tendencies, sometimes appearing in the lives of boys and girls who have said "yes" to Jesus.

This morning we're going to study the "harmful and objectionable habits" of weeds. One of the bad characteristics of the weed is its ability to multiply at a rapid rate. One plant of hedge mustard is capable of maturing over one-half million seeds in one season! Imagine one plant having that many babies! A tumbleweed can throw about 200,000 seeds in one year. If you have lived in the West you will know of the interesting way in which the tumbleweed throws its seeds. When the seeds are "ready" the tumbleweed pulls up its roots and starts rolling over the land. As the wind carries it along, the seeds are scattered over a wide territory. Since the tumbleweed has nearly 200,000 seeds to scatter, it can do a great amount of damage.

Sin spreads rapidly from city to city. We'd almost think that sin was like a tumbleweed, scattering evil deeds all over our land. The Bible says: "Our transgressions are multiplied before thee, and our sins testify against us" (Isa. 59:12). The increase of crime in the United States proves the fact that sin can multiply. If sin is allowed to live in your life, it will take root and multiply. Your first sin may be minor, such as disobedience to parents. In later life you'll find it easy to disobey the law and get yourself into serious trouble. If any of you know that you have sin in your life, ask Jesus to remove it before it starts multiplying. "I acknowledged my sin unto thee, and mine iniquity have I not hid. I said, I will confess my transgressions unto the Lord; and thou forgavest the iniquity of my sin" (Ps. 32: 5).

Many weeds have a fibrous root system. These roots branch out in all directions, forming a dense mass of fine rootlets. If you were to dig up certain weeds like the pigweeds, lamb's quarters, or common nightshade, you'd see the many roots. These roots remove moisture and food from the soil, cheating the good plants of the water and minerals that they should receive. The weeds also cheat the good plants of light, and of space. They have the bad habit of crowding out the plants that are needed for food.

Sometimes boys and girls allow sin to crowd out the blessings that they should receive from God. It is through Bible study and prayer that you receive food from God; and sin can keep you from getting this food. The Bible says: "Study to show thyself approved unto God, a workman that needeth not to be ashamed, rightly dividing the word of truth" (II Tim. 2:15). If you are not reading your Bible, you're being cheated. The Word of God also says, "Men ought always to pray" (Luke 18:1). You're being cheated a second time, if you allow the Devil to keep you from praying.

We mentioned that weeds take sunshine from the good plants. Many weeds have broad leaves, which enable them to steal most of the light away from the good plants. If you say that you are a Christian and carry sin in your life, you are hiding the Light of Christ from others. The Lord may be saying, "Ye are departed out of the way; ye have caused many to stumble" (Mal. 2:8). The Bible says: "Let your light so shine before men, that they may see your good works, and glorify your Father which is in heaven" (Matt. 5:16). "If we walk in the light, as he is in the light, we have fellowship one with another, and the blood of Jesus Christ his Son cleanseth us from all sin" (I John 1:7).

Weeds have the ability to adapt themselves to a wide variety of soil and climatic conditions. They are not "choosy" on the type of soil, because they can grow almost anywhere. They also have the ability to live through drought, while the good plants die. Sin is not "choosy" in whose heart it grows. It thrives in the hearts of either the poor or the rich. Some hearts are more "fertile" for sin, because of the lack of proper early training; and these boys and girls, many times, become criminals.

Weeds act differently in certain localities. Wild carrot (Queen Anne's Lace) is not as bad in Europe, from where it came, as it is in certain parts of the United States. There are places in the West where the wild carrot has taken possession of entire fields. Liquor may take possession of a man's complete life, making a drunkard of him. Another man may drink without becoming a drunkard. He may, however, injure his health. Thus, the same sin may grow differently in certain hearts. Cigarette smoking may cause the death of one man, while it may only slightly injure another man. The sin of gambling also acts differently on the lives of men. Some men actually steal in order to have money for gambling. If you boys play marbles "for keeps" you have allowed the sin of gambling to enter your lives.

You may have heard people say that there are some weeds that are good to eat. They refer to the dandelion, which can be used as greens. Sin is also made to appear as being good. Have you heard the radio announcer say that cigarettes were good for one because they calm the nerves? Have you heard the radio voice tell you that liquor was good because it provides an appetite? Sin may have the appearance of being good, but when you check into it, you'll find out that the badness is covered up.

Sometimes weeds are planted in gardens because of their beautiful flowers; but they soon get out of hand and wear out their welcome. The gardener then has a difficult time getting rid of the bad plant. Because of its attraction, a certain sinful habit may be picked up and allowed to grow in the heart. This habit sometimes gets out of hand, and then the "victim" will say, "I wish I could get rid of it!" You may have heard someone with the cigarette habit making a remark similar to this one. It's a good idea to keep sin from attracting your attention. Keep it completely away from your life.

Some weeds, when young, resemble good plants. There are times in which the gardener may find it difficult to distinguish between the weeds and the radishes, when either of the plants first appear. Sin also has ways of fooling people. The Bible says: "Take heed to yourselves, that your heart be not deceived, and ye turn aside" (Deut. 11:16).

There are men who give their lives to the study of weeds. It's their job to think up ways of removing the bad plants from the fields. Jesus Christ gave His life to remove sin from the world. Jesus can take all the sin out of your life. He has made a study of you and knows just what you should do to get rid of sin. Here is His suggestion: "If we confess our sins, he is faithful and just to forgive us our sins, and to cleanse us from all unrighteousness" (I John 1:9).

Lesson 12

MOSSES

OBJECTS NEEDED: Moss specimens.

Although mosses are very common, we give them little attention. We walk over them in the forests, hardly knowing that they are there. These plants are unusually small, with the tallest of them being less than five or six inches. They do not have real leaves, although their "substitutes" perform the work of leaves very well.

As we think of the characteristics and habits of this plant, we could call Mr. Moss by the name of Mr. Sinner. Now, I know that will surprise you, because mosses are such beautiful and delicate plants we hate to attach such an uncomplimentary name as Mr. Sinner. However, this morning we are not using the beauty of the plant—we're using its characteristics and habits.

First of all, Mr. Moss likes dark and shady places. The Bible says: "Men loved darkness rather than light, because their deeds were evil" (John 3:19).

More crime is committed at night than in the daytime, because the evildoers find that darkness is a help and shield to their deeds.

Mr. Moss looks beautiful from the top. His velvety appearance and various hues of green make him an enchanting plant. But what is he covering up? Maybe it's a rotten log or a dead stump! Let's remember an evil heart may not be visible from the outside. When you walk into a store you cannot tell which of the "customers" is a thief. Neither can the store owner know who is a shoplifter. Evil thoughts are also easily covered up. Your friends do not know what is in your mind, but God knows what is there. The Bible says: "The Lord seeth not as man seeth; for man looketh on the outward appearance, but the Lord looketh on the heart" (I Sam. 16:7). "I the Lord search the heart . . . to give every man according to his ways, and according to the fruit of his doings" (Jer. 17:10). There have been times in which you have disobeyed your father or mother, and you covered your actions so that they would not know of your deed. You may have done as good a cover-up job as does Mr. Moss. The Bible says: "He that covereth his sins shall not prosper: but whoso confesseth and forsaketh them shall have mercy" (Prov. 28:13). Punishment from God does not come from confessing your sins—it comes because you do not confess them.

Mr. Moss does not have real roots. He has a flat network that spreads over the surface he is covering. You can see the network in the moss that we have here. We read in the Old Testament of the sins of a group of people known as Israelites. God punished many of them severely. But God spared a few of the "uprooted people" for He says: "And the remnant that is escaped of the house of Judah shall yet again take root downward, and bear fruit upward" (II Kings 19:30). God can give you deep roots that really grow down into fertile Christian soil and you will bear fruit. You don't need to have a shallow network of roots like the moss has.

Mr. Moss does not bear flowers or produce seeds. He has a way of multiplying by dustlike spores which drift from the plants. These dustlike spores are so tiny that we do not see them when the plant throws them into the air. An evil person can commit sin without anyone seeing his crime. There are times in which crime becomes visible only when it is put through a "microscope" of testimony by other people. Even then the crime is so well covered up that the police have a difficult time to make it visible enough for punishment.

We do not read of Mr. Moss as being very useful. We think that a plant should serve as food or be used as medicine. There are thousands of sinners who are of no use to this world. They make the world more evil and a less desirable place in which to live. If you are a sinner and have never accepted Jesus as your Saviour, you can accept Him now. You can say: "For I acknowledge my transgressions: and my sin is ever before me. Wash me throughly from mine iniquity, and cleanse me from my sin" (Ps. 51:3, 2).

If you have already accepted Jesus as your Saviour, but you have not completely taken sin out of your life you may need to say: "Purge me with hyssop, and I shall be clean: wash me, and I shall be whiter than snow" (Ps. 51:7).

Lesson 13

FERNS

OBJECTS NEEDED: A collection of ferns. If possible, have a "fiddlehead" sprout and also the full-grown leaves.

The fern is one plant that has a past. Many, many years ago the ferns grew so tall that they resembled trees. They filled the swamps and valleys; and when they died the pressure of sand and mud changed the plant material. The altered "remains" are known as coal. Fossil imprints of ferns, and other plants, have been found in the coal beds. You can see these fossil ferns at a museum.

The ferns are a higher type of plant than the mosses. They have leaves, called fronds, which are capable of manufacturing food. These leaves may be three or four inches long, or they might be as much as six feet in length. The largest ferns, some of which are as much as fifty feet high, are found in the tropics.

Most of the ferns have leaves that die in the fall.

70

In the spring new shoots appear which some people call "fiddleheads" because they resemble the scroll end of the violin. These little fascinating curls gradually unroll and spread out into a fern.

Not only does the fern have leaves that manufacture food, but it also has roots and stems. Thus, the ferns are not as "low" a plant as the mosses, but neither are they in the class with the higher plants, because they have no flowers and no seeds. They have a way of making new plants by spores. We can say that they are on the dividing line between the low and the higher class of plants.

There are boys and girls who have given their hearts to the Lord, but have not completely stepped over to God's side. They still want to rule their own lives, allowing sin to come in occasionally. They are not classed as "low" because they have taken the first step—that of giving their hearts to the Lord. But they are not in the "higher" Christian bracket because they have not dedicated their lives to the Lord, allowing Him to rule in their hearts completely.

Ferns are large and showy. Their dainty and delicate leaves have given them a prominent place in flower arrangements. They, however, are of little value to man, other than being decorative. They are of very little use as food and medicine, although occasionally people will eat the fiddleheads when they first come up.

The ferns remind us of a certain class of people in the church. They are the "showy ones" who are of little help to the minister. They like to be in the "spotlight" where people will notice them. Many times their lives are not what they should be and they are poor witnesses for the Lord. These showy people could be called the "self-centered" ones, who still have not surrendered the big "I" in their lives to the Lord. The fern has no fruit; and the showy Christian also bears no fruit. He is not interested in winning others to Christ—he is interested in exalting himself. "Pride goeth before destruction, and a haughty spirit before a fall" (Prov. 16:18).

Why not dedicate your life to Christ, asking Him to remove the undesirable traits that keep you from being a fruitful Christian? Step completely over on God's side and you'll be happy for it.

Lesson 14

MUSHROOMS

OBJECTS NEEDED: Mushrooms taken at random from the woods.

Today we're going to talk about a plant that lives on the dead. Our subject will be mushrooms.

These mushrooms are white, indicating that they have no way of making their own food. They lack the substance called chlorophyll which is the green coloring matter found in plants. They are the scavengers of the vegetable world for they live upon dead wood and leaves. There are a few mushrooms, however, that live on growing trees.

Mushrooms have their best growth in the autumn, especially after a good shower. The leaves and branches then contain plenty of moisture, offering the plants an excellent feast.

As we look at our collection of mushrooms, we notice they are not alike. Most of them have a stem with a cap upon it resembling an umbrella. Under the umbrella are plate-like growths called gills. Beneath the gills, attached to the stem, is a ring, generally called the collar.

There are certain kinds of mushrooms that can be eaten, but there are some species that are very poisonous. Those who know very little about mushrooms do not pick the ones found in the woods using them for food, because these plants may be poisonous.

This morning we want to talk about these deadly mushrooms—the ones that may cause death if eaten. The poisonous mushrooms resemble the good ones, and many of us do not know the difference between the two.

Sometimes the Devil presents bad habits in such a manner that they appear good. There are times in which he even shows himself as being good. The Bible says: "And no marvel; for Satan himself is transformed into an angel of light" (II Cor. 11:14). His true nature is really that of a roaring lion. "Your adversary the devil, as a roaring lion, walketh about, seeking whom he may devour" (I Peter 5:8).

In order to make sure that you don't get poisoned from deadly mushrooms, you have to refrain from eating them. That's simple, isn't it? You can use the same principle in handling the Devil. If you stay away from him, he can't harm you. You shouldn't even peek over his fence! The Bible says: "Neither give place to the devil . . . lest Satan should get an advantage of us: for we are not ignorant of his devices . . . Submit yourselves therefore to God. Resist the devil, and he will flee from you" (Eph. 4:27; II Cor. 2:11; James 4:7).

Don't let the Devil have an interview with you. Stay close to Christ, where you will be protected from the Devil's poison.

Lesson 15

FUNGI

OBJECT NEEDED: A bracket type of fungi that is found on trees and stumps.

Today we're going to talk about something that appears dead and yet is alive. You may have noticed the shelf-like growths that appear on tree trunks, old logs, or stumps. We have picked one of these fungus growths and we'll use it in our lesson for today.

This queer growth of nature has no stems, roots, or flowers; nor does it have any leaves. Because it has no leaves and cannot make the green coloring matter, called chlorophyll, it must steal food from its neighbors. The neighbor that this plant uses is a tree, a stump, or an old log.

There are people who think they can take a Christian experience from someone else. You cannot depend upon your mother or your father for your Christian food. The Bible tells us: "All have sinned, and come short of the glory of God" (Rom.

3:23). When you accept Jesus as Saviour, He starts feeding you through prayer and Bible reading. You will not have to depend on others for your spiritual food, because you can attach yourself to Christ and draw your food from Him.

This fungus that I have here is of no use to mankind. We can't eat it, nor can we feed it to the animals. The church member who tries to take spiritual food from others instead of becoming a Christian and getting the food from Christ is of no use to God. This kind of a church member cannot win others to Christ because he has nothing in his heart.

This bracket type of fungus is easily marked. By using a sharp stick we can place our initials on it. The writing will become brown in a very short time. You do not need to detach it from the tree or stump in order to write upon it. When I picked this plant it was white on one side but now it is brown. I have handled it several times which may have caused it to lose its original color.

If you are not grounded in the Bible, the Devil will try to mark your life, causing it to become discolored. The original whiteness disappears. He may even try to write his name on you. The Bible tells us to fight the Devil by using Bible quotations. The Devil thought Christ would be an easy "mark" when he found Him in the wilderness. He tempted

Jesus three times, and on each occasion Jesus used the term: "It is written" (Matt. 4:4, 7, 10). The Devil is afraid of the verses in the Bible and you can defeat him by quoting them. It is therefore very important that all Christians become familiar with the Bible so that they will not be an easy "mark" for the Devil.

When the bracket fungus is attached to a living tree, it can do much damage. In fact, it can kill the tree. It starts growing in an injured place in the bark, extending its fungus threads into the heart of the wood. Sin also does much damage in the life of a boy or girl. It sends its poisonous threads into the heart, causing evil deeds, bad thoughts and unkind words to develop. "Their thoughts are thoughts of iniquity; wasting and destruction are in their paths" (Isa. 59:7).

As we've already said, the bracket fungus has no flowers and bears no fruit. Boys and girls, living in sin, yield no fruit for God. They win no one for Christ. I hope that none of you are of the fungus type. If you have sin in your life, Jesus can remove it. Are you willing to say with the Psalmist, "Search me, O God, and know my heart: try me, and know my thoughts: and see if there be any wicked way in me, and lead me in the way everlasting" (Ps. 139: 23, 24)?

Lesson 16

OAK GALLS

OBJECTS NEEDED: Oak Galls. Use both the hard type and the soft ones that appear on the leaves. The galls can be found on the ground during the winter months.

Sometimes the oak trees suddenly develop abnormal growths resembling the malignant tumors that are found in the human body. These enlargements are called galls. We have two kinds before us this morning. These little balls have been the home of an insect. If we look closely, we can see the tiny hole through which the insect let itself out of its house. In the spring the insect lays the eggs on the oak leaf. When the larva hatches, it begins to eat into the leaf. A substance is discharged that eventually forms a soft house. As we look at this leaf upon which there is a gall, we notice how fragile the house is that was built by the insect. Many people refer to this type of a gall as an "Oak Apple." Sometimes the oak trees are full of these galls; and then they resemble a tree loaded with apples. You wouldn't enjoy eating one of these apples. Now, let's take a look at the hard galls. The hard oak balls are formed on the stems and not on the leaves. These galls are woody and not a bit fragile. Sometimes these hard apples will stay on the tree for more than one season. Not until the stem breaks off will the hard oak apple disappear.

The galls are harmful to the oak trees. An oak tree is beautiful when its leaves and stems are not covered with the harmful balls. The insect that makes the gall is an enemy to the tree. So long as the enemy is flying around the tree, it does no harm. It's when it gets into the tree to build a home that it becomes harmful.

The Devil does not harm us unless he moves into our lives and is allowed to dwell there. The Bible says: "Neither give place to the devil . . . lest Satan should get an advantage of us: for we are not ignorant of his devices" (Eph. 4:27; II Cor. 2:11). You may ask the question, "How does the Devil get into me?" He lives in your life through bad habits and sinful deeds. God can get the Devil out of your life. "Submit yourselves therefore to God. Resist the devil, and he will flee from you" (James 4:7).

This oak gall destroys the beauty of the leaf. Sin can also destroy the beauty in your life. If you continue to serve the Devil, your health could be ruined. Also, you could lose your friends by the bad words you'd speak and the sinful deeds that you'd do. Listen to what the Bible says: "Neither is there any rest in my bones because of my sin. For mine iniquities are gone over mine head: as a heavy burden they are too heavy for me. . . . I am troubled; I am bowed down greatly; I go mourning all the day long. For my loins are filled with a loathsome disease: and there is no soundness in my flesh" (Ps. 38:5-7). When we read these verses in the Psalms, we are astonished at the destruction that can do to the body.

The oak gall is a fascinating thing to view, but should remember that it's a harmful thing. sin appears as a fascinating thing, but remember that it's deadly. The Devil has to get you to indulge in sinful habits. that cigarettes are not harmful—he to you that they taste good and are nerves. The Devil also says, paper advertisements, that liquor Cigarettes and liquor may be people, but let's remember they le says: "In whom the god d the minds of them which of the glorious gospel of God, should shine unto Devil can get you to take up unclean habits, he is blinding your mind.

Trees were not made to be a home for gall flies. Neither was your life created by God as a dwelling place for the Devil. God wants to live in your life, making His home with you. The Bible says: "Know ye not that ye are the temple of God, and that the Spirit of God dwelleth in you? And what agreement hath the temple of God with idols? for ye are the temple of the living God; as God hath said, I will dwell in them, and walk in them; and I will be their God, and they shall be my people" (I Cor. 3:16; II Cor. 6:16).

Wouldn't you like to have God living in your life? Being a Christian is really fun. Why don't you try it!

Lesson 17

AUTUMN LEAVES

OBJECTS NEEDED: An assortment of colored autumn leaves. Place a green leaf in a small jar and cover it with alcohol. The alcohol will pull out some of the chlorophyll.

In the fall the leaves turn to a beautiful color and then drop to the ground. The tree then takes a vacation from work.

When we studied leaves, we learned that the green coloring matter was called chlorophyll. The beautiful yellows and reds that we see in the fall are present in the leaves all the time. When the leaves stop working, the green disappears. We can prove this fact by placing a green leaf in a small container filled with alcohol. In a few days the alcohol will start turning green because it has pulled some of the chlorophyll out of the leaf. If the leaf is allowed to remain in the alcohol long enough, it will become an autumn leaf. Instead of being green, it will be yellow, or whatever pigment of autumn coloring that the leaf holds. Thus, we see that the green covers the beautiful autumn colors, and only when the green is removed, can we see the true beauty of the leaf.

You may have Christian beauty in your life, but it is covered up. Jesus can remove the coating of sin that keeps you from being a radiant Christian. If you confess your sins, Jesus can remove this coating. You need to say: "I acknowledged my sin unto thee, and mine iniquity have I not hid. I said, I will confess my transgressions unto the Lord; and thou forgavest the iniquity of my sin" (Ps. 32:5). You have to die to sin, just as the leaf had to start dying before any autumn coloring became visible. After Jesus has removed the sin you can "worship the Lord in the beauty of holiness" (I Chron. 16:29). Your friends will also see the Christian beauty that has been uncovered when your sins are removed.

Lesson 18

ACORN

OBJECT NEEDED: Oak twig with acorns hanging on it.

This acorn is the trademark of the oak tree. No other tree produces acorns. If we are in doubt as to whether a tree is an oak or not, we only need to look for acorns on the tree or on the ground underneath it.

For a few minutes let's think of the word "trademark." The dictionary defines it as "a symbol used in connection with merchandise, and pointing distinctly to the origin or ownership of the article to which it is applied." In this definition we notice two thoughts. (1) It has a connection with merchandise and (2) it points to ownership.

As Christians we are the "trademarks" of God. We have a connection with a merchandise—that of salvation for the world. We also point to our owner—God. The acorn comes from the oak tree—the Christian comes from Christ. When God allowed us to be called *Christ*ians He permitted us to take the name of His Son. Are you a true "trademark?" Do you really represent Christ?

This acorn has a cap, which is a protection to the seed. Christ "is our help and our shield" (Ps. 33: 20). This cap on the acorn holds the seed to the tree. The oak is one of the strongest of all trees. We never see an oak uprooted by the wind. The acorn seed is attached to something very strong—its parent oak. And the cap is the thing that holds the seed close to the tree. God is like a sturdy oak, with Christ being the attachment that brings us to God. We cannot come directly to God. We can only come close to Him through Christ. God is pure, and we cannot appear in His presence without having our sin removed. This thought is expressed in that favorite verse: "For God so loved the world, that he gave his only begotten Son, that whosoever believeth in him should not perish, but have everlasting life" (John 3:16).

I want you to notice how tightly the cap holds the seed. Not until the seed is ripe does the cap release that part of the acorn. This acorn is still green and needs the food from the oak: therefore, it must stay attached to the cap. Christ holds the "green" Christian tightly to Him. The new child of God needs food—he needs instruction, and he needs to be strengthened.

When the acorn is ripe, the cap allows the seed to drop to the ground. The seed is then sent on its mission—to produce another oak tree. After Christ has trained us, he releases us for service. He expects others to become Christians through our witness.

The acorn has to be planted before it can produce. The squirrel is the best acorn planter. God is our planter. He places us for service in a location approved by Him.

Sometimes acorns do not get planted. Because the seed is sweet it is used for food by certain animals. There are many sweet believers who have not been "planted" for full-time Christian service. Because of their "sweet" lives, they provide food for the weaker Christians. A "sweet" Christian is one with a good disposition, who has kind thoughts, and is helpful to others.

Whether you become a full-time worker for Christ or just a witness day by day, you are God's seed, placed upon this earth to produce for Him.

Within this small acorn is the power to become a huge oak tree. Within your life there is God's power to make you a strong worker for the Lord. The Bible says: "Now the God of hope fill you with all joy and peace in believing, that ye may abound in hope, through the power of the Holy Ghost" (Rom. 15:13). It is possible for you to have this power.

If you are willing to acknowledge your sin, asking God to take you as His child, you can be in a position to ask for the power that we have mentioned. Just as the acorn has potential power, so you can have power. Your power comes by allowing the Holy Spirit to dwell in your life each day.

Lesson 19

SOIL

OBJECTS NEEDED: A jar full of rock particles, another one full of sand and a third jar of good soil. Also, have a few larger stones.

This morning we're going to find out what makes soil. In my hand I hold a rock. Some day it may be turned into soil. Our soil originally came from rocks. Many of the mountains have been cut down by water, intense heat, freezing weather, glaciers and lichens. Sand that is blown against a mountain by the wind can wear away the hardest rock. We have a good example of the power of sand driven by the wind when we look at the rainbow bridges and other formations in the deserts in the western part of the United States.

When the rock wears down, it may be crumbled into rock particles like that I have in this jar. When the rock particles become decomposed they turn into sand. Sand becomes mixed with dead leaves, roots and stems of plants. In this bottle I have soil taken from the garden (or woods). In this soil there are many living creatures. These creatures are called soil bacteria—they are the earth's clean-up squad. When dead plants and animals are placed in the soil, the bacteria start to work. It causes decay to occur, thus adding valuable chemicals to the soil.

Sometimes soil gets "sour" and then the farmer spreads lime over his land. He may add chemicals of various kinds to improve the soil. The ground must have air or plants cannot live in it. Any soil that is packed down, with little air in it, is considered poor soil. The soil should also have an occasional rest. It can be worked to death just as easily as a human being. God taught the Jews to rest their land every seven years (Lev. 25:3-5).

In connection with our study of soil, we're going to use the parable found in Matthew 13. (Read to the class Matt. 13:3-8.) As we read this story we noticed four kinds of sowing. The first seed fell on top of the soil, where the birds picked it up. The Bible doesn't say that the soil was bad. It says that the seed was laid in the wrong place—it was laid on top of the ground and was never turned under. If you have lived on a farm you will know that the crows sit in a tree waiting to pick up any of the seeds that do not get turned under. The Bible gives the following interpretation for this kind of sowing: "When anyone heareth the word of the kingdom, and understandeth it not, then cometh the wicked one, and catcheth away that which was sown in his heart. This is he which received seed by the way side" (Matt. 13:19). If you hear the Gospel story and do not allow it to take root in your life, the Devil may come and take the "seed" away from you.

The second kind of sowing is that of placing seed in stony places where there isn't much earth. Suppose we planted seeds among the stones and rock particles like the sample we have in this jar. Do you think the seed would grow well? Seeds planted among rocks cannot get a chance to root like they should. When the sun comes up it scorches the plants and they die. The Lord gave the following interpretation of this kind of sowing: "But he that receiveth the seed into stony places, the same is he that heareth the word, and anon with joy receiveth it; yet hath he not root in himself, but dureth for a while: for when tribulation or persecution ariseth because of the word, by and by he is offended" (Matt. 13:20, 21). You may know of some boy or girl who accepted Jesus as Saviour; but when a playmate called him a "sissy" because of the decision, the Word of God was allowed to die in the heart. I hope that the Gospel is well rooted in your lives so that your friends who are not Christians cannot uproot the Gospel that you have received.

The third sowing was done among the thorns. If you have ever made a garden you know how fast the weeds grow. If they are not removed they will choke the good plants. A thorn is classed as a weed. Jesus explained this as follows: "He also that received seed among the thorns is he that heareth the word; and the care of this world, and the deceitfulness of riches, choke the word, and he becometh unfruitful' (Matt. 13:22). Bad habits can keep young people from serving God the way that they should. They choke out the good seed that Christ has sowed in the heart.

The fourth sowing was done on good ground. The soil was excellent and the planting properly done. Some of the seed brought forth "an hundredfold, some sixtyfold, some thirtyfold" (Matt. 13:8). Jesus explained it as follows: "But he that received seed into the good ground is he that heareth the word, and understandeth it; which also beareth fruit, and bringeth forth, some an hundredfold, some sixty, some thirty" (Matt. 13:23).

Your heart is the ground into which the Gospel seed is planted. Are you allowing the seed to grow, bringing forth a harvest of good works? In order for the seed to grow you will need to remove all sin from your life. The Bible says: "Create in me a clean heart, O God; and renew a right spirit within me" (Ps. 51:10). A clean heart makes good soil for the growing of the Gospel.

Are you providing good soil for God's planting? He can make you into an outstanding Christian if you'll yield your life completely to His will.

Lesson 20

THE RIVER

OBJECTS NEEDED: A piece of cardboard about ten
or twelve inches long and about five inches wide.
A shallow pan and a water pitcher. A small
amount of sand that contains a few pebbles. The
cardboard is folded lengthwise so that it forms
a U-shaped trough. (A piece of metal can be used
instead of the cardboard.)

I'm sure there isn't a person in this room who
hasn't seen a large river. You, no doubt, have seen
it in the summer time when the water was low and
the current moving slowly. You may have seen the
river in the winter time when it was overflowing
its banks. Almost every winter, some part of the
United States becomes flooded. At flood stage many
things are pulled along with the river. Sometimes
homes and other buildings are taken in its swift
flow.

A river is capable of picking up stones, sand, logs
and other things, and carrying them long distances.

A river need not be at flood stage in order to transport material. The next time you stand upon the banks of a river or stream, see how many things you can count that the river is moving. The stones and sand on the bottom of the river will be invisible as they move; but you can see the logs, leaves, seeds, and branches move down the stream. On the Oregon Coast there is a place called Boiler Bay. The name was attached to this location because the ocean brought in a boiler from a wrecked boat and deposited it in the bay. The ocean and large rivers are capable of moving huge articles.

We could not bring a river to class today, but I am going to demonstrate how water can move sand, and gravel. Here we have a pitcher of water and a jar of sand. Mixed with the sand are a few small pebbles. We're going to place the material from the jar into this trough and then we'll pour a small amount of water over the top. Notice, how the water moves some of the sand down into the pan. When I pour the water slowly, it will move only the sand, but when I pour it fast, even the pebbles will move. Thus, you can see that a rapidly moving stream is capable of moving heavier articles than a slow, sluggish body of water.

We're going to let the water represent the Gospel. Christ told the woman at the well, "Whosoever drinketh of the water that I shall give him shall never thirst; but the water that I shall give him shall be in him a well of water springing up into everlasting life" (John 4:14). This trough will be the world and the sand and pebbles will be the people that need to receive the Water of Life. The pan will be Heaven. In order for these people in the trough to get to Heaven, they will have to be taken there by the Gospel, which is represented by the water in the pitcher.

Let's see how the people of the world receive the Gospel. The Bible tells us, "Whosoever shall call upon the name of the Lord shall be saved. How then shall they call on him in whom they have not believed? and how shall they believe in him of whom they have not heard? and how shall they hear without a preacher?" (Rom. 10:13, 14). We're going to use the term "preacher" to represent anyone who tells the Gospel to some unsaved person. The person may be a preacher, but he could also be a Sunday school teacher, or a radio speaker. This "preacher" could be your mother or your father. He could also be you! When you tell other boys and girls about Jesus, you're as much a preacher of the Gospel as the minister in the pulpit. The Gospel is in the world and so are the unsaved people. God needs someone to pour the Gospel onto the people so that they will be saved and pulled into Heaven.

When I poured the water on this material slowly,

only the sand moved into the pan. Sometimes we do not give out very much Gospel and then only a few people are saved; but when we really pour on the Gospel, we push the hard-to-get unsaved person Heavenward.

If you have given your heart to Jesus, you're a worker for Him. He expects you to invite other boys and girls to Sunday school. He expects you to act like a Christian when you are playing with your friends. You should be unselfish and never take toys away from others. You should also say kind things and never display anger. If you have a bad temper, the Lord will remove it from your life if you will let Him.

In the Old Testament there is a story of a boy by the name of Samuel. God called Samuel to work for Him. He was only a small boy, but, nevertheless, God knew He could use him. Let's read what happened when God called: "And the Lord came, and stood, and called as at other times, Samuel, Samuel. Then Samuel answered, Speak; for thy servant heareth. And the Lord said to Samuel, Behold, I will do a thing in Israel, at which both the ears of every one that heareth it shall tingle" (I Sam. 3:10, 11).

God can use you, if you will tell Jesus you want to help Him.

Lesson 21

RAPIDS AND WHIRLING WATER

OBJECTS NEEDED: A quart jar, filled half full with sand, pebbles, and a few small sticks. Place enough water in the jar to fill it about two-thirds full.

Today we're going to talk about rapids and whirling water. We, of course, couldn't bring the river with us, but we can illustrate the motion by the equipment that we have before us.

When you go swimming in the river, you are told to stay away from rapids and whirling water. Rapids are generally so powerful that a boy or girl can easily be knocked down even in shallow water, and then carried into the deeper water. Whirling water has an undercurrent that sucks downward. When your father goes fishing, he watches out for either of these two types of water.

When a stream of water comes down a steep

mountainside, there is much swirling and washing. All the loose sand and rocks are moved down the stream with the water. The steeper the hill, the more active the water becomes. The river dashes the large boulders, trying its best to get them out of its way. A churning stream of this kind is very dangerous.

Today we have with us a jar filled with soil and water. There is sand, pebbles, and a few short sticks in this soil. We're going to shake the jar. Notice how fast the contents are moving. The sand, the pebbles and the other material are all constantly churning while I'm shaking the jar. When I stop shaking it, the material starts to settle and the water quits moving.

This morning I want to talk to you about forgiving and forgetting wrongs that come your way. Have you ever had some one do an unkind deed to you and then you kept churning it around in your mind? So long as you kept the wrong moving in your mind, you could not possibly forget it. You might tell it to your friends and they too would keep "churning" the wrong around by telling it to someone else. A river that keeps dashing rapidly can be dangerous; but so are bad thoughts in your mind, if you keep "churning" them around.

The Bible says: "Where there is no talebearer, the strife ceaseth . . . A froward man soweth strife:

and a whisperer separateth chief friends . . . He that repeateth a matter separateth very friends" (Prov. 26:20; 16:28; 17:9). When you repeat a wrong to someone else, you may be separating two friends. It would be much better to forgive the person who has wronged you, and then forget the matter so that it does not get passed on to someone else.

If you forgive the boy or girl who has wronged you, you can be of help to him. He may not be a Christian, and if you show a forgiving spirit, he may be impressed enough to want to become a Christian also. The Bible says: "Ye ought rather to forgive him, and comfort him, lest perhaps such a one should be swallowed up with overmuch sorrow" (II Cor. 2:7).

You should be willing to forgive other boys and girls, for Jesus has forgiven you for your bad deeds. And if Jesus had not forgiven you, Heaven would not be your future home. There is a sentence in the Lord's prayer that we repeat many times: "And forgive us our debts, as we forgive our debtors" (Matt. 6:12). The sentence really means, "forgive us our wrongs, as we forgive those who wrong us." Would you want the Lord to forgive you in the manner in which you forgive your friends? The Bible says: "And be ye kind one to another, tender-hearted, forgiving one another, even as God for Christ's sake hath forgiven you" (Eph. 4:32).

When I stopped shaking this jar, the water quieted down. If you will forgive and forget the wrong that someone has done to you, the matter will soon disappear from your mind and also from the mind of the person who wronged you. Your life will be quieter and so will that of the other boy or girl. If you are carrying a grudge against someone, why not forgive him and forget it?

Lesson 22

STONES[1]

OBJECTS NEEDED: Since agates, jaspers, and petrified stones are found in many rivers, these can be
included in the selection. There should, however,
be one good-sized stone of questionable mixture.
These stones should contain dust or a small
amount of mud upon them.

Today we're going to look at one of God's creations that has proved to be a wonderful collector's
item—stones. Stones can be found in all parts of
the world. Some of them are precious, while others
are just plain stones that have been taken from the
river.

Here is a very common stone—the river is full of
them. Let's remove the dirt by giving the stone a
bath. The water brings out the color and now it's
rather pretty. Notice the bands that seem to be
cemented together to form the stone. This rock
reminds me of a "down and out" person who needs

[1]Reprinted with permission of *Christian Life* magazine,
Chicago, Illinois.

to have his life cleansed by the blood of Christ. Immediately after the cleansing the color in the life appears and God has formed a new person from a faded and sinful character.

Here is a stone (agate) that is more beautiful. This stone is clear and if it weren't for the dust upon it, we could look straight through it. Let's give it a bath, too, and see how it looks. This stone reminds me of a person who has never gone into deep sin. The Bible tells us that *"all* have sinned and come short of the glory of God" (Rom. 3:23). And even one small sin can keep a person from Heaven. Because of this one sin, this person also needs to be washed in Christ's blood.

Now here is a pretty red jasper. (Any vivid stone will do.) Let's wash it and see how it appears. The color is brighter than before because the water brings out the luster. This stone reminds me of the "nice appearing" person—the society person. But even the society person needs to be cleansed in Christ's blood. Now that we have washed the jasper we'll place it beside our agate.

The next stone is a petrified one. This stone has gone through some hard testing but it has come through in its beauty. Let's wash it and take a look at it. Hardships never admitted anyone to Heaven and so this person must also be covered by Christ's blood.

While I have been talking, the first stone has become dry and has lost its luster. When we dip it again into the water, the luster returns. But if the stone were permitted to dry again, it would once more lose its bright appearance. We could keep dipping the stone into the water as fast as it dries, but that would be a nuisance. There is one other way and that is to keep them in the water, so let's place all the stones in this pan of water.

Suppose we use our imagination a little and pretend these stones are Christians, washed in Christ's blood. The pan will represent the Bible. Each boy and girl can be cleansed daily by the reading of the Word. The Bible says: "Ye are clean through the word which I have spoken unto you" (John 15:3. See also Eph. 5:26, 27). The Bible teaches you how to live each day so that you will keep your Christian sparkle.

Lesson 23

Fossils

OBJECTS NEEDED: Plant and animal fossils.

Closely related to our study of rocks is that of fossils. A fossil is the ancient remains of an animal or plant preserved in rocks. The word "fossil" comes from a Latin word that means "to dig." Because of the meaning of the word, we generally think of digging when we think of fossils. The geologists have done much digging, since fossils reveal something of the past—the climates, and the distribution of plant and animal life.

Coal is one product that we receive from ancient plants. These plants grew in the swamps millions of years ago. When they died, other plants grew on top of them. Layers of sediment filled in over the decaying plants. The decayed plant material, in due time, became coal. In many of the coal beds we can see leaf prints, revealing the type of plants that grew at that time of history.

Our museums contain many excellent fossils.

Some of these fossils are large animals of the past. If it were not for the fossils of dinosaurs we would not knowing anything about these large and vicious-appearing animals of the long ago. The museums also contain specimens of sea life; some of these fossils having been found upon mountains a long ways from any sea or ocean. We know that water must have covered these mountains, otherwise the sea fossils would not be there.

When we go fossil hunting we expect them to be in certain places. For instance, we generally find them in sandstone, shale or limestone. Christians are expected to be found in Christian places. Jesus does not want his children to be in questionable places of amusement.

Fossils tell us a story of the past—a story that took place many, many years ago. These plants and animals, if they could speak, could tell us interesting things. They, however, do tell us many things relating to the past. They have left for us the imprint of their lives. God expects us to leave an "imprint" of our lives when we leave this earth. Men, like D. L. Moody, have left their "imprint" upon the lives of the men and women that they have won for Christ. Christian authors have left their "imprint" by the books that they have written.

None of us need to wait until we're dead to

leave an influence. We can have an influence on those with whom we associate each day. Let's look at a few of the things that we can do. First we should be witnesses by the way we act. The Bible says: "That ye may walk honestly toward them that are without" (I Thess. 4:12). We should live honest Christian lives, being witnesses to them who are without the Gospel. The way we act is more important than what we say. You have heard the saying: "What you do speaks so loudly that I cannot hear what you say."

In the verse that we just read I want you to notice that the word "walk" is not spelled with a *"t,"* making the word "talk." If we talk to someone about Jesus and we do not live a good Christian life, that person will not be impressed at what we say. The Bible says: "Ye are our epistle written in our hearts, known and read of all men" (II Cor. 3:2). Someone wrote a much-quoted verse as follows:

> We are the only Bible
>   The careless world will read;
> We are the sinner's gospel,
>   We are the scoffer's creed;
> We are the Lord's last message
>   Given in deed and word—
> What if the line is crooked?
>   What if the type is blurred?

God expects us to tell others of the Gospel after

we have cleaned up our lives. The Bible uses the term: "Sound speech, that cannot be condemned" (Titus 2:8). If our lives are pure before all people, then they cannot condemn us. "Let your light so shine before men, that they may see your good works, and glorify your Father which is in heaven" (Matt. 5:16).

Now, we come to the speaking part of witnessing. Have you gone through the day without speaking to someone of Jesus? Have you invited someone to Sunday school? Have you told someone of the protection that Jesus gives you each day?

You have heard of men leaving a memorial behind when they die. The memorial might be a church which they have paid for, or it might be equipment for a church. These memorials are like fossils that are left behind so that others may become Christians.

The best imprint to leave for the following generation is a dedicated Christian life—a life that influences children, grandchildren, great-grandchildren. You can start building this kind of a life now. Your imprint can even now be seen by the pupils and teachers in your school. You should start to build that kind of a Christian life *now*, so that it will have a long influence.

Lesson 24

SNAIL

OBJECT NEEDED: A snail's shell.

The snail travels slowly. But why should he be in a hurry? Since he carries his house with him all the time, he never has to hurry home. Whenever any one doesn't move as fast as we think he should, we say he is moving at a snails's pace. We find Christians who move that way, too. The preacher may try his best to get certain members to do work in the church, but they take their time responding. Sometimes boys and girls do not respond very well when mother or father speaks to them. Don't be like a snail when you're asked to do something. Jesus likes his children to be good Christians in the home.

The snail's house is a shell. It serves as a protection from the enemy. Whenever the snail has an undesirable caller, he crawls inside his shell and shuts the door. This may not seem very polite, but it sometimes saves his life. Whenever the Devil comes near us, Jesus offers protection. The Bible says: "He hath said, I will never leave thee, nor forsake thee" (Heb. 13:5).

The snail has no backbone. His flabby body isn't attached to bones of any kind. There are many boys and girls who seem to have no backbone because the Devil hasn't any trouble in getting them to follow his suggestions. Christians should never listen to the Devil. The Bible says: "Submit yourselves therefore to God. Resist the devil, and he will flee from you" (James 4:7).

The shell that the snail carries around is heavy for him to lug everywhere he goes. It seems to be a burden to the snail. Sometimes boys and girls have unsaved parents and friends who become a burden to them. A deformed body or poor health can be another type of burden. Jesus can carry these burdens. "Cast thy burden upon the Lord, and he shall sustain thee; he shall never suffer the righteous to be moved" (Ps. 55:22).

The snail leaves a mucous trail when he moves. You may have seen this shiny trail in the woods. Every Christian makes a trail for someone to follow. That trail should be a "shiny one" so that it may easily be seen. What kind of a trail are you making? Do your friends know that you are a Christian by the life you live? Let Jesus have full charge of your life and then you'll be the kind of a Christian who will influence others.

Lesson 25

BIRD NESTS

OBJECT NEEDED: A bird nest. If clay is available, make three egg-shaped balls and paint them blue. The nest can be gotten in the fall or winter after the birds leave for the South. It should not be taken in the spring when it is in use.

We sometimes refer to the nest as being the home of the bird, but we should call it the nursery. Most birds only use their nests in which to raise their babies, and then they abandon them.

Some birds show remarkable skill in building their nests. The most beautiful are those made by the Oriole. The nests made by these birds could win a prize in any Birds' State Fair. The crudest nests are those of the cuckoo or the mourning dove. Let's look at the nest that we have before us and see what material the bird has used. (Name the material, which may be grass, sticks, twigs, bits of string, paper, mud, horsehair, or moss.) Some birds are very careful of what they build their home.

111

As Christians, are we as careful of what material we use in the building of our character? The material to use in building a good Christian life is: love (Mark 12:30, 31), purity (Matt. 5:8), self-denial (Luke 9:23), steadfastness (I Sam. 12:21), zeal (Ps. 42:1), consecration (Rom. 12:1), humility (Matt. 18:4) and meekness (Matt. 5:5).

In many instances the material used in the nest will identify the bird that built it. For instance, the robin uses mud, the bush-tit likes feathers, and the chipping sparrow uses horsehair. The material that we put into our lives identifies us as Christians or as sinners. Our actions and our words tell on us; and our friends will know on what side of the fence we're living.

The birds build their nests on three different levels. There are many that build on a very low level. The pelican, the gull, the killdeer, and many others place their nests on the ground. The nests that are laid upon the ground are in a dangerous place. They could be crushed by feet (Job. 39:13-15). The people who build their lives on a low level are in a dangerous position. A "low life" always contains sin, and God will not allow anyone to enter Heaven with unforgiven sin in his life. God is willing to remove the sin. The Bible says: "As for our transgressions, thou shalt purge them away" (Ps. 65:3).

There are birds that build their nests in trees and under roofs (Ps. 104:17). These nests are in a safer location because they are higher. When we ask God to forgive us of our sins, He places our life on a higher level. We're now above the mire and mud of sinful pleasures.

There are birds like the eagles, that build their nests upon the high cliffs (Job. 39:27-29). When we've had our sins forgiven and our life has been placed upon a higher level, God comes to us with the invitation to "come up higher." Our response should be: "Lead me to the rock that is higher than I, for thou hast been a shelter for me, and a strong tower from the enemy" (Ps. 61:2, 3). The closer we live to our Lord, the more protection we will receive when the Devil tries to tempt us.

If you are living on the ground level, ask God to move you up by forgiving your sins and taking you as His child. If you are a Christian, why not dedicate your life to God, asking Him to give you a higher and closer walk with Him?

Lesson 26

FEATHERS

OBJECTS NEEDED: Feathers. (Tail feathers from the chickens in the barn yard or long feathers from the birds in the timber.)

Before we look closely at the feathers that we have this morning, let's allow our minds to go back to the time in which quills were used for pens. The men would cut the tip of the feather to a point and then use it as we would a steel pen. Of course it could not be filled with ink; but it, nevertheless, wrote fairly well. (You can demonstrate how the quill worked, by cutting one of the tips into the shape of a steel pen point. A word or two could be written with the quill.)

Did you ever stop to think that your life is like a book, which people read? The writing is not done with a quill or a steel pen. Your actions are the words that appear in the book. Some people never read the Bible and thus cannot know that Christ died for their sins. They have to read about Christ through *your* life. The Bible says: "Ye are our epistle written in our hearts, known and read of all men. Forasmuch as ye are manifestly declared to be the epistle of Christ ministered by us, written not with ink, but with the Spirit of the living God; not in tables of stone, but in fleshly tables of the heart" (II Cor. 3:2, 3). The writing that your life is doing may cause one of your friends to become a Christian. If your life is what Jesus would want it to be, someone will be impressed. We can then say that you are doing a good job of writing. But if your life is not the kind Jesus would want you to live, you may cause someone to stay away from the church. They may say, "Look at John—he says he's a Christian and I saw him cheat!" (Do not use a name from the class.) If you're that kind of a Christian, you're doing a poor job of writing.

I want you to notice how the barbs of this feather spread out, almost like a fan. As a Christian, you too have to spread your godly influence. If you keep the Gospel to yourself, no one else will hear of it. The Bible says: "Go ye therefore, and teach *all* nations" (Matt. 28:19). Spread, spread, and spread—that's what Jesus expects you to do with the Gospel.

The bird is the only creature that wears feathers. The feathers serve the same purpose as do our clothes. They are a covering for the body of the bird. You, no doubt, have seen chickens with their feathers removed. Don't they look queer! One time there was a woman who could not bear to cut the chicken's head off, so she chloroformed the bird. She picked the feathers off and laid the chicken on the table. When the bird "came to" it started walking around. Imagine how it looked in the "nude." God gave the birds feathers to keep them warm and dry. The feathers overlap each other so that the rain cannot enter and reach the body. Have you ever noticed how the chicken droops its tail when it is out in the rain? The water runs off its body better when the tail is in that position. Young chickens are covered with what we call "down." "Down" is a feather without a quill. The "down" is fluffy, and is the young bird's woolen underwear.

We have learned that the feathers are a covering and a protection for the bird. Jesus is our protector. He is always with us to protect us from harm. God says: "Fear thou not; for I am with thee: be not dismayed; for I am thy God: I will strengthen thee; yea, I will help thee; yea, I will uphold thee with the right hand of my righteousness" (Isa. 41:10). Temptation and hardships can rain down upon us, but our God will protect us.

The birds give themselves an oil bath. They have a small bag of oil on the top of their tail. They reach under their feathers, and get some of the oil in their bill. They then pull their feathers through their bill and the oil gets on the feathers. How would you like to work that hard in order to take a bath? When we think of oil, as mentioned in the Bible, we think of anointing. Saul was anointed when he was selected as king (I Sam. 15:1). There were other kings which followed Saul who were also anointed for service. When you were a small child, your parents may have had you dedicated. At that time the minister may have anointed you with oil.

Many feathers are used for ornamental purposes. There was a time when birds were killed for their feathers. These feathers were placed on women's hats. We do not kill birds nowadays for their feathers because it's against the law. Birds should not be killed for any reason! Sometimes chicken feathers are dyed and used on hats. When we think of an ornamental feather we think of an ornamental Christian. An ornamental Christian is only a church decoration—not a church worker. God wants us to work for Him and not to sit and fold our hands. You boys and girls can work for your church by inviting others to Sunday school, and by being good Christians on the playground.

There are many feathers that are naturally beautiful, the peacock being a good example of a bird with beautiful feathers. The China Pheasant of Oregon is also a colorful creature. We probably should ask the question: "Is beauty useful?" We could also ask the question: "Is beauty necessary?" There are many Christians who are not beautiful physically. Spiritually they are beautiful. Their beauty is made up of good deeds and words. When God looks at you, can He say that you are a beautiful Christian?

This feather is very light in weight. Not only is it hollow, but it is also made of very light material. The feathers have to be light in weight so that the bird can fly. If the feathers were heavy they would weigh the bird down. If we allow sin to weigh us down we will not be able to go high with Christ. The Bible says: "Let not sin therefore reign in your mortal body, that ye should obey it in the lusts thereof . . . For sin shall not have dominion over you" (Rom. 6:12, 14).

The chicken sheds its feathers once a year. It looks very shaggy with so many of its feathers gone. How do you think the Christian boy or girl would look if he shed his Christian habits, his Christian love, and his Christian kindness? To God, that boy or girl would not be very attractive. I'm sure the world would not consider him attractive either.

Let's go back for a moment and look over the features of the feather. (1) It at one time was used as a writing tool. Your life is like a book with chapters being continually added. Is the writing good or

is it bad? (2) The feather spreads out and serves as
a covering for the bird. We, as Christians, should
spread the Gospel; and in turn, Christ is our covering—our protector. (3) There are ornamental
church members just as there are ornamental feathers. These believers are only interested in outward
beauty, and not the inward kind. God wants to
anoint all His believers so that they will be workers
and not just church decorations. Can God count
on you to follow in the path that He has made for
you? Can He count on you to work for Him? To
witness for Him? To love Him?

Lesson 27

DRIFTWOOD

OBJECTS NEEDED: Pieces of driftwood appropriate for flower arrangements. Also, weird formations that appear to have no special use.

As we walk along the beach of an ocean or lake, we see large piles of driftwood. Some of the pieces are small, like the ones that we have before us, while others are huge. Some of the pieces have been churned and washed by the water until they have taken weird forms. These peculiar shapes fascinate people so much that they pick up the pieces of driftwood, taking them home. Many of the pieces can be used for decorative purposes. Housewives use novelty pieces in their flower arrangements. A rumpus room can be decorated with driftwood, giving it a marine atmosphere. Sometimes the boys and girls pick up the pieces on the beach, forming driftwood animals with them. Even in spite of the fact that driftwood gets picked up, the majority of the pieces remain on the sand, marring the beauty of the beach.

There are two points we want to discuss in relation to driftwood. When we think of the word "drift" we are reminded of someone who won't "stay put." This person drifts from one job to another, or from one idea to another. We think of these individuals as those who are not to be trusted with responsibility.

God has boys and girls upon whom he cannot depend. They drift in and out of Sunday school. Sometimes they are present, while other times they are spending the day elsewhere. They may say they are Christians when they are with the church group; but when they are with worldly friends, they actually deny their Lord. They shift "with the tide," as we might term it. If you are drifting, without an anchor in Christ Jesus, let God help you to get your feet on solid spiritual ground where you can serve Him.

Because of its white, smooth appearance, driftwood has been called Mother Nature's dry bones. As you know, dry bones are "good for nothing." They are dead, dead, dead. The Bible says: "O ye dry bones, hear the word of the Lord . . . behold, I will cause breath to enter into you, and ye shall live" (Ezek. 37:4, 5). If you are not the kind of a

Christian you should be, Jesus is able to put new life into your dry spiritual bones. You will then be alive and working for Him.

Lesson 28

CONIFERS
(THE CHRISTMAS TREE) [1]

OBJECT NEEDED: A decorated Christmas tree.

The conifers are trees with needle-like leaves that remain green throughout the year. These trees are very popular at Christmas time. We could say that the conifer is one of the symbols of Christmas. Many people, however, do not see Christ in their tree. Let's take a look at this decorated tree and see if we can find anything that reminds us of Christ.

Most people have to buy their Christmas trees. We, too, are purchased with a price. The Bible says: "For ye are bought with a price: therefore glorify God in your body, and in your spirit, which are God's" (I Cor. 6:20). The price is Jesus Christ who died on a cross to buy our salvation.

We notice that our Christmas tree has a fresh green color. The color of green reminds us of life—

[1]Reprinted by permission of the *Sunday-School World,* published by The American Sunday-School Union of Philadelphia.

life everlasting. Christ is the only person who has
had unending life, for He has always existed and always will exist (John 1:1, 2). Some day we will go
to live with Him forever, if we are His children.

There must be some preparation necessary before
a tree can be ready for the best corner of the living
room. A stand should be placed on the tree. After
that, the "rain," the balls, and the lights are put on
the tree. God began to prepare the tree of salvation before the foundation of the world. Before the
world began God planned that we should be saved
(Eph. 1:3-5).

On this tree we see some glittering streamers
which we call "rain." This looks very nice upon a
Christmas tree, but the fact is, the foil is of very
little value. We can buy enough for a tree with
only a few pennies. God's salvation is much more
valuable. It can't be purchased at any price. In the
book of Acts, we find a man who thought he could
buy salvation with money, but he was told that this
was not possible (Acts 8:20). There is no false
glittering in God's salvation as there is in the decorations on a Christmas tree.

On this tree there is a red ball. The color of red
speaks of Christ's blood, shed to cover our sins. This
blue ball reminds us of Heavenly things. Here is a
silver ball and also a gold one. These remind us of

God's wealth. We should remember that the world, all that's in it, belongs to God.

Electric lights of various shapes and colors are placed on Christmas trees. A light removes darkness. Christ, the Light of the World, can remove the darkness from any heart. If you have the darkness of sin in your life, let Jesus remove it from your heart.

When we have the tree decorated, we place our presents under the tree. God gave the first Christmas present. It was His Son. Since then, people have been giving presents to each other without a thought of giving a present to God. Your life is the best present you can give to God this Christmas season.

A Christmas tree affords much pleasure to those in a home. There is something joyful about it. Christ wishes us to be as joyful as were the shepherds and Wise Men of old when they found Him. Sin brings unhappiness; but Christ brings joy to the heart. This joy cannot come until the sin is removed from the heart.

If you have never given your heart to Christ and known the joy of sins forgiven, why not do it now in this blessed Christmas season?

INDEX TO BIBLE REFERENCES